ARCHAEOLOGY

JEAN COOKE

Topics

All the words that appear in **bold** are explained in the glossary on page 30.

Cover: Life-sized pottery figures found in the grave of Emperor Chin Shih Huang Ti.

First published in 1986 by
Wayland (Publishers) Ltd
61 Western Road, Hove
East Sussex BN3 1JD, England

© Copyright 1986 Wayland (Publishers) Ltd

British Library Cataloguing in Publication Data
Cooke, Jean
    Archaeology. – (Topics)
    1. Archaeology – Juvenile literature
    I. Title   II. Series
    930.1   CC171

ISBN 0–85078–827–7

Phototypeset by
Kalligraphics Ltd, Redhill, Surrey
Printed and bound in
Belgium by
Casterman S. A.

Contents

What is Archaeology?

If we want to know what happened in the past, the first thing we usually do is to read what people wrote at the time – their own stories of events, letters, bills or even old wills. But people have been writing things down for only about 5,000 years, and even during the period of written history there are great gaps in our knowledge.

Hieroglyphics, a form of writing in pictures used in Ancient Egypt.

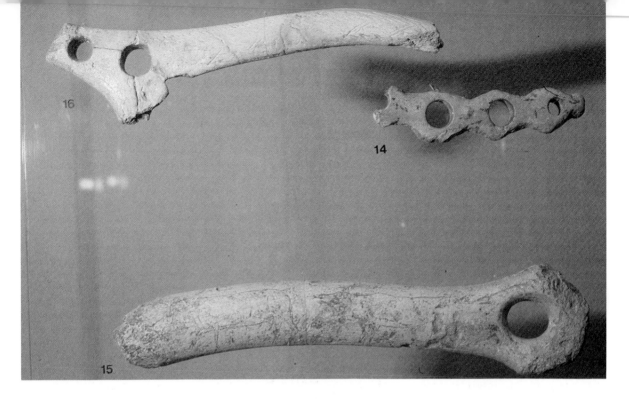

Archaeologists learn about the lives of Paleolithic people by studying these engraved bone-handles from that time.

Archaeology is the art of finding out about the past by examining ancient clues when there is no written history to help us. So archaeologists are historical detectives. The word 'archaeology' comes from a Greek term meaning 'the discussion of ancient things', but what archaeologists are really studying are the lives of the people who made and used those things.

Quite often archaeology proves that stories nobody really believed about the past are, in fact, true. For

Heinrich Schliemann, the first man to find the ruins of Troy.

example, the Greek poet Homer wrote a long account of the siege of Troy, which he called *The Iliad*, after another name for the city, Ilium. Most people thought it was just a story until about a hundred years ago, when a German scholar called Heinrich Schliemann, dug up a mound in north-western Turkey and found the ruins of Troy – and clear signs that it had been destroyed after a fierce battle.

Archaeologists have to keep careful records of everything they find, because digging into a **site** usually means destroying it. There is no second chance of detecting clues that were missed. Many of the early archaeologists were careless, digging away in their search for 'treasure' rather than trying to piece together a picture of life many years ago. One of the first

An artist's idea of what a Bronze Age village looked like, based on finds made by archaeologists.

Thomas Jefferson, later President of the United States, was a keen archaeologist.

Below *A huge stone head, found in Mexico. It was carved by the Olmec Indians.*

scientific archaeologists was Thomas Jefferson, later President of the United States. He explored an American Indian burial mound in 1784, and carefully noted everything he saw.

Modern archaeological skills were developed by a retired British army officer, Lieutenant-General Augustus Pitt-Rivers, in the 1880s and 1890s, and by Sir Mortimer Wheeler, forty years later.

On Site

When a building decayed and fell down in the past, people just used to level off the site and build a new one on top of the ruins. If this happened many times, that piece of land became a series of layers, each newer than the one below. The ancient site of Troy is made up of the ruins of nine cities, one on top of another. Such a site is a real

Nine cities were built at Troy, one on top of another. Homer's Troy was number seven.

The temple at Delphi in Greece. This site has been fully excavated.

historical dustbin, and the fragments found in each layer can tell us something about the people who threw them away. So archaeologists must dig up a site very carefully, stripping off one layer at a time.

A properly excavated site is a very busy place. First of all it has to be measured and **surveyed**. The first actual digging is usually a trench right across the site. Workers use spades and wheelbarrows to move large amounts of soil. The colour of the soil generally changes between one

A surveyor measures distances and angles so that an accurate map of the site can be plotted.

All objects are labelled carefully.

layer and another, and these changes show up on the sides of the trench. A dark patch may indicate that a wooden post used to be there and has rotted away. Such patches are called **postholes**. Postholes show where a wooden building once stood.

For a more detailed inspection, people work on their hands and knees, scraping the soil away with small trowels, a little at a time.

When they come to a **find** – an object that might be of interest – they may use tiny brushes and even dentists' instruments to clean it without disturbing it. They often leave an important find in the ground for a time to try to see where it fits in with the other objects in the soil.

The finds are collected in trays and plastic bags, then sorted and labelled. There is usually a photographer on the site, and someone to make sketches showing where objects have been discovered.

A worker uses a dental probe to scrape soil away from a skeleton.

This Greek vase dates from around 700 BC. Archaeologists can often say what shape a vase was from a few fragments.

Many **artefacts** rot away to nothing, but pottery does not rot, even if broken into small pieces. People have studied the shapes of pots over the years. They can often identify a fragment and say roughly when it was made, and what kind of society was present on the site at that date.

Working under Water

Archaeology is often carried on under water, as well as on dry land. The wrecks of many ships lie under the sea. Seawater can preserve materials such as wood, which might rot away in the ground. The mud or sand of the sea-floor preserves them even better. For example, the Dutch **East Indiaman** *Amsterdam* ran aground on the beach near Hastings, in southern England, in 1748. The ship settled into the sand to a depth of about 9m (30 ft). Although the waves have pounded away the upper part, three-quarters of the ship, protected by the wet sand, still remains, together with its cargo.

Underwater archaeology is much more difficult and expensive than working on land, and it can be cold,

The wood of this wrecked ship has been preserved by sand and mud.

Divers may only be able to work on a wreck underwater for a few minutes at a time.

dark and dangerous. Divers have to
go down to the wreck, but they may
only be able to work there for a few
minutes at a time. If the wreck is
near the shore the water can be
very murky, so a diver is lucky to be
able to see more than one or two
metres away.

Using an airlift, a diver can quickly suck up sand and any small objects from the sea bed.

Divers work from a ship or platform close to the wreck site. This is their base which carries all the tools and gear. One useful tool is the **airlift**. It is a large tube which the diver can move about the sea bed. It works like a vacuum cleaner, sucking up sand and small objects quickly. There have been some very exciting discoveries. In

1961 the Swedish warship *Wasa* was raised from the depths of Stockholm Harbour, where she sank in 1628. In 1982, the remains of Henry VIII's warship *Mary Rose*, which sank in 1545, were lifted from the sea-bed off Portsmouth. The wreck of a more modern warship, the ironclad US

A picture of the Mary Rose *painted in about 1546. Today her remains are in a covered dock at Portsmouth, England.*

MERRIMAC.   MONITOR.

A drawing of the Monitor (right) before she sank during the American Civil War.

Monitor, which fought an important American Civil War battle in 1862, was found off the coast of North Carolina in 1973.

Some people working on sunken wrecks are only interested in trying to **salvage** their cargo. Gold and silver from several pirate ships have been brought up in this way, including many of the famous coins called 'pieces of eight'.

Stumbling on the Past

Archaeologists generally have a good idea where to look for suitable sites to dig up. In an old town, pulling down a building is likely to reveal something of interest beneath where it stood. Some sites show up from the air, like those of many of Britain's seven thousand or so 'lost' or abandoned villages. But some of the most

Sometimes what seems to be a heap of stones on the ground shows up as a site from the air.

19

interesting discoveries have been made totally by accident.

One day in 1947, Muhammad Adh-Dhib was looking for a lost goat. Muhammad was a **Bedouin** shepherd boy, herding his animals on the shores of the **Dead Sea** in Palestine. High up a cliff face he noticed a small cave, and climbed up to explore it. There he found a number of pottery jars, and inside some of them were hidden ancient

It was in one of these caves above the Dead Sea that the Dead Sea Scrolls were found.

scrolls. These were the famous 'Dead Sea Scrolls', some of the oldest Hebrew **manuscripts** ever discovered.

Another lost animal, this time a dog named Robot, was responsible for a remarkable find – the prehistoric **cave paintings** of Lascaux in south-western France. The dog vanished down a hole in the hillside while chasing a rabbit. A boy who was with the dog scrambled into the hole – and there he found the cave, with its wonderful paintings of animals.

This cave painting of a bull and a horse at Lascaux was made in prehistoric times.

21

Working on the Roman Road at Icklesham.

An unknown Roman road was uncovered in the English village of Icklesham, thanks to the efforts of a young boy in 1978. Knowing that his grandmother was digging near her house in search of a Roman iron furnace, he went into her vegetable garden with his bucket and spade – and found traces of Roman activity. Three years later local archaeologists decided to dig a little further, and so discovered the old road.

A group of Chinese villagers digging a well in the valley of the Yellow River came across an exciting find in 1974. It was the grave of Ch'in Shih Huang Ti, the emperor who built the Great Wall of China in about 200 BC. The grave covers an area nearly as big as a football pitch, and it contains 6,000 full-sized pottery figures of soldiers.

In 1985, a farmer in Bulgaria was digging a ditch in his garden, when he unearthed a hoard of silver-gilt bowls, jugs and other vessels, made around 300 BC.

A life-sized pottery soldier and horse from the tomb of Emperor Ch'in Shih Huang Ti. There are 6,000 figures in the tomb.

Some Famous Discoveries

Possibly the most romantic discovery of all time was the tomb of Pharaoh Tutankhamun, the boy-king of Egypt who lived about 3,300 years ago. Two British archaeologists, the Earl of Caernarvon and Howard Carter, spent eight years looking for his grave. It was the only royal Egyptian tomb that had never been robbed. They found it in 1922 in the Valley of the Kings, near Luxor. It was full of more than 1,700 treasures, including chariots, statues, thrones and shrines. The boy-king's mummified (preserved) body was inside a solid gold coffin. More details of Tutankhamun's times are waiting to be pieced together after the discovery in 1986 of what is thought to be the tomb of his minister, Maya.

The Step Pyramid at Sakkara in Egypt was the first pyramid ever built.

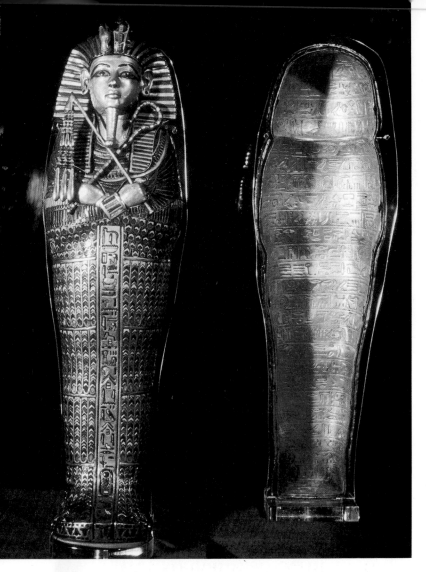

A beautifully decorated miniature coffin from the tomb of Tutankhamun.

Another royal tomb was discovered in Greece in 1977. It was the grave of Philip of Macedon, father of Alexander the Great, who lived 2,300 years ago. It contained two golden **caskets**, and some bronze armour that probably belonged to Philip.

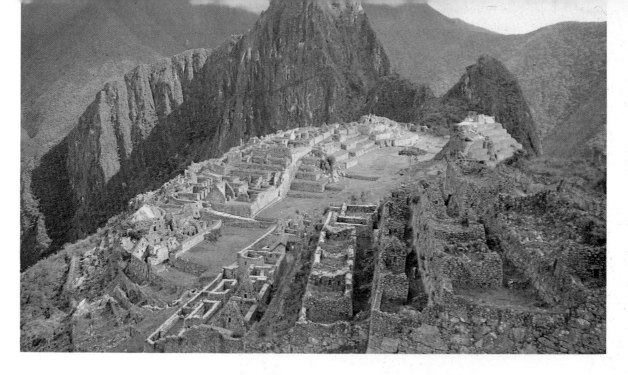

The deserted town on Mount Machu Picchu, the retreat of the Inca people.

Archaeologists have been able to prove that America's history is much older than people suspected. In 1983 the foundations of what is probably the oldest building in the Americas were discovered in Chile. They may be as much as 15,000 years old.

An Icelandic **saga** told how a Viking named Leif Ericsson sailed west to a land which he called Vinland, because of the vines and grapes he found there. Leif made his voyage in about the year AD 1000. People thought this was just a story – but in 1963 the remains of a Viking settlement were found in Newfoundland.

The Incas, an American Indian people, ruled Peru and lands near it before the Spaniards conquered them in the early 1500s. A legend told how the Incas retreated to a hideout in the mountains. In 1910 the American explorer Hiram Bingham set out to find this hideaway. Near the mountain of Machu Picchu he discovered a deserted town, containing buildings made out of huge blocks of granite.

This skull, found in Johannesburg, is female and thought to be three million years old.

In Asia, French explorers found a lost city in the jungles of Kampuchea in 1860, abandoned since the 1400s. It contains a vast temple called Angkor Wat covering about 2.6 sq km (1 sq mile).

Another lost city was the Roman town of Pompeii, near Naples in Italy. It was wiped out by the eruption of the volcano Vesuvius in AD 79. Excavations there have been going on since 1748.

Archaeology is not just for the experts. Although they have the skill

Examples of Roman pottery and wall paintings at Pompeii.

Hand-axes like these date from prehistoric times.

and patience to interpret new finds, anyone may be fortunate enough to notice unusual features while on a country walk. **Crop marks** in a field could show the site of long-forgotten ruins just below the surface.

A plough might turn up pieces of broken pottery from a deserted village or even a prehistoric hand-axe. If you find anything like this that interests you, tell your local history society or museum about it. You might start off another important archaeological investigation.

Glossary

Airlift A device like a giant vacuum-cleaner for sucking sand from underwater wrecks.

Artefact Any object made by people.

Bedouin A member of a band of Arab people who roam the deserts of south-western Asia and North Africa.

Casket A small box, generally used to hold valuable items such as jewellery.

Cave paintings Paintings made by prehistoric people 20,000 years ago or more, on the walls of caves in many countries, including France, Spain, South Africa and Australia.

Crop marks Places where plants grow faster or more slowly than the surrounding crops. Dark green may indicate a ditch or well underneath; parched, yellowing grass could show the line of stone foundations or an old road.

Dead Sea A very salty lake that lies between Israel and Jordan, 397 metres (1,302 ft) below sea level.

East Indiaman A large sailing ship, used for trade between Europe and the East Indies.

Find Any object found during an archaeological dig, especially a small one.

Manuscript Any document or book which is written by hand (that is, not printed).

Posthole The hole in which a wooden post once stood, which shows as a darker patch of soil.

Saga A long story, usually told in verse.

Salvage To save a vessel or cargo from loss at sea.

Scroll A roll of parchment or paper inscribed with writing – the ancient way of making books.

Site Any place where an archaeological dig is in progress.

Surveyed To have plotted a detailed area of the ground to show where digging should be carried out.

Books to read

*Archaeological Guide and
    Glossary* by James Stewart
    (Phoenix House, 1960)
Archaeology by Jean Cooke and
    Others (Sampson Low, 1976)
Archaeology from the Earth by Sir
    Mortimer Wheeler (Penguin,
    1964)
*Collins Field Guide to
    Archaeology* by Eric S. Wood
    (Collins, 1964)
Roman Roads by P. Warner
    (Wayland 'Eyewitness History'
    series, 1980)
The Mary Rose by Margaret Rule
    (Conway Maritime Press, 1983)

The Vikings by T. Richard
    (Wayland 'Living History'
    series, 1986)
The Vinland Sagas, *The Norse
    Discovery of America* translated
    by Magnus Magnusson and
    Herman Pálsson (Penguin, 1965)
The Wreck of the Amsterdam by
    Peter Marsden (Hutchinson,
    1974)

Note: *The National Geographic
Magazine* often has articles on the
latest archaeological discoveries.
Ask your librarian about it.

Picture Acknowledgements

Ancient Art and Architecture Collection 19 (B. Norman); Stephanie Colisanti
9; Robert Harding Picture Library cover; Hastings Area Archaeological
Research Group 22; Mansell Picture Library 8; Mary Rose Trust 15,16, 17;
Marion Morrison 26; Peter Newark's Western Americana 8; Photri 18;
Theodore Rowland-Entwistle 24; Ronald Sheridan 4, 5, 6, 10, 11, 13, 20, 21,
23, 25; Mick Sharp 10, 12; Wayland Picture Library 7, 14, 22, 29; Werner
Forman Archive 8, 28.

Index